a
Mixed
Bag

a Mixed Bag

"A look at life as I see it"

MAY PARK

Harp Presss

First printed 1999
Reprinted 2009

Published by

Harp Press
18 Stephen Road
Bexleyheath
Kent, DA7 6EE
England

ISBN: 978-0-9537141-0-0

Printed in England by Booksprint

DEDICATION

*I dedicate this book to my Spirit Family:
Mum and Dad and my brothers, Tom and
Derek.*

*I would like to thank them and all my
friends and helpers for their, inspiration,
support and encouragement throughout.*

*Special thanks must go to my friend Alf, for
nagging, nurturing and nudging me on
when I faltered. Without his help, this book
would not have come to fruition.*

MAY PARK.

May is the youngest of nine children and with eight brothers she has always considered life a "Mixed Bag". Devoted to her parents, she was deeply shocked at the death of her father when she was eight years old.

Educated at Westwood Secondary Modern School for Girls, Drama, Maths and English were her favourite subjects, and all influenced her career and leisure. She was a bookkeeper during the early years whilst caring for her family and helped run her husband's roofing business for eighteen years. She was a student of a creative writing group known as "The Shrewsbury Writers" for twelve years, and helped to edit, print and collate their magazine. She was co-editor of the "Sheltered Grapevine", a magazine for the elderly residents in the fourteen Sheltered Housing units in Dartford, where she worked.

May is a singer comedienne and enjoyed entertaining with "Co. '80" Old Time Music Hall Group from 1987 till 2003. She writes most of the material used in her act, performing original songs and odes at local clubs, theatres and charity concerts. Many of the songs and carols she has composed have been performed by schools and used at churches that she supports. May is a member of "The Bob Hope Theatre" and has performed numerous leading and supporting roles for the group.

Being a family person, May is proud of her two sons Michael and Jeffrey, and her grandsons, Shaun, Ryan and Daniel.

Also an accomplished speaker May won a National Speech Contest in 1997 with a speech inspired by Princess Diana, for whom she had great regard. She enjoys giving light-hearted talks to women's institutes and other organisations, mostly using her own material.

When asked, "Have you had a book published?" She always replies "There's one in the bag!" This selection has come out of that bag.

CONTENTS

FRIENDSHIP

Friendship is a golden tree
With branches everywhere.
Its blossoms can enrich the soul
And gently scent the air.
Its leaves offer protection
From whatever may befall.
Its roots are strong,
Its fruit is sweet,
And waiting for us all.

BOOK OF LIFE

Each day we write a new page
In the 'Book of Life'.
Funny days, sunny days,
Sad days filled with strife.

Each day when it is written,
Leaves a memory to relish,
So try to make those memories
Ones that you can cherish.

Each twist and turn along life's road,
Will bring a challenge new,
But how you meet them,
Greet or beat them,
Is entirely up to you.

A PRAYER

God, we often use Your name
And not always in prayer.
Sometimes we take for granted
That You are always there.

When worries fall upon our heads,
The way they're apt to do,
We seek the strength and wisdom
We can only get from You.

So look on us with mercy, Lord,
Guide us day and night,
Help us find the glow of hope
And bathe within its light.

Amen.

DO YOUR BEST

Do your best
For that is all that man can ask of you.
Pay attention!
Concentrate on everything you do.

When tasks grow hard or heavy
Or begin to be a bore,
Proceed with perseverance
Trying harder than before.

If you give your greatest effort
You still may fail the test.
But you can say with hand on heart,
"At least I did my best".

BE GRATEFUL

When you've reason to be grateful,
Don't be afraid to say.
Just offer up a word of thanks
When good things come your way.

Prayers come all too easily
When filled with grief and woe,
But when those prayers are answered,
Acknowledge it is so.

Gratitude costs nothing,
It does not warrant pay,
And good turns passed along to friends,
Will all return someday.

So do not keep them to yourself,
For they grow with every share,
But always spend a moment,
On a 'thank you' prayer.

FIGHT ON.

It's easy surrendering to despair
Self pity and bitterness too,
When, with a little effort
You could be smiling through.

>Why burden yourself with misery,
>Dwelling on the past?
>The present time is fleeting
>With the future looming fast.

Every life has dark clouds,
Dimming the brightest sky,
But a drop of rain, a puff of wind
And those clouds go scudding by.

>So always try to make each day
>A happy and memorable one
>Loaded with love and laughter
>Filled with joy and fun.

Face adversity with a grin,
Surround it with love and light.
Be grateful for blessings, however small,
And never give up the fight.

A BETTER PLACE

There is a far, far better place
Awaits us all some day.
Where the grass is always lush and green
And the skies are never grey.

Where all the birds sing sweetly,
The sunsets glow with gold.
The summers never grow too hot,
Nor the winters grow too cold.

All who enter in there
Find the meaning of true peace.
The crippled are made fit and well,
Each tortured soul released.

So when we've done our stint on earth,
With the good Lord's love and grace,
We all will find eternal life,
Within that heavenly place.

WEAR YOUR POPPY WITH PRIDE

Wear your poppy with pride, friend,
For those who fought and died.
They fell on the field of battle,
Weapons of war at their side.

They had no stomach for killing.
They had no desire to die.
They stood on the field of battle
Sometimes just wondering "why?"

Often their limbs were aching and cold,
Hunger pangs filled them with pain,
But they stayed on the field of battle
Defending again and again.

For some the war was a short one,
They were injured, diseased or they died.
They fought on the field of battle
With bodies of friends at their side.

They died on the field of battle,
For a cause that could not be denied.
They won us a peace and freedom.
So wear your poppy with pride.

TREE

A tree grows strong and handsome,
With branches open wide.
It knows its worth upon this earth,
Its burdens are its pride.

It puts the heat into a grate,
It supplies the bars across a gate,
It makes the table for a plate,
These burdens are its pride.

It screens us from the midday sun,
Can make the toys that bring us fun,
Provides our coffin when day is done,
These burdens are its pride.

Yet never does it once complain
When battered by the wind or rain;
It simply bends to take the strain,
Then it straightens up again,
And does it all with pride.

If we could model on that tree,
What better people we would be.

HELPING HANDS

Everyone needs HELPING HANDS,
A good friend is a must.
The sick, the poor, the lonely
All need someone they can trust.

The sick, in mind or body,
Their limbs all wracked with pain,
Have the need of helping hands
To make them well again.

The poor man, when times grow hard,
With bills upon the shelf,
Needs helping hands to guide him,
To save him from himself.

The depressed, lost and lonely soul,
Prisoner of his fate,
Desperately needs helping hands
Before it is too late.

No man is an island,
For God is always there.
Yet even He needs helping hands
To demonstrate His care.

So open up your hearts, my friends.
Show that someone understands.
The sick, the poor the lonely,
Every one needs HELPING HANDS.

SANDS OF TIME

Golden are the sands of time,
But how soon their minutes ebb,
Each second is a work of art,
A precious, silken web.
    Our stay on earth is only short,
    With so much knowledge to be sought,
    And many lessons to be taught,
    Before the sands run out.

All souls have a destiny,
Tasks they must complete,
For some the way is light and bright,
While other's drag their feet.
    Bestowed with blessings from on high,
    The power of love and hate are nigh,
    Sometimes they falter, but still must try,
    Before the sands run out.

Life's highway has its twist and turns,
Its rocky hills to climb,
So never waste a single grain,
Of your golden time.
    Live life to its fullest,
    Then you'll know without a doubt,
    You've done your best to attain your goals,
    Before the sands run out.

I SPOKE TO THE LORD

I spoke to the Lord and He answered me,
Freeing me from all my fears.
I told him of my pain and grief
And he wiped away my tears.

I spoke to the Lord of my problems,
The large ones and the small.
He gave me the will to continue
And the strength to cope with them all.

I confessed to the Lord I was lonely
And sometimes close to despair.
The Lord said:
"I am the truth, I am the life,
And I am always there."

HEALING PRAYER

Dear Lord
We come to You again,
For those in sickness and in pain,
They need Your strength,
The will to cope,
They need to find a little hope.
There are so many everywhere,
Who need Your loving and Your care.
We send our prayers for them, tonight,
To ask You make their darkness bright.
That You will send down
Your great love,
To glow upon them from above.
And if You have some left,
We pray,
A little of it comes our way.

Amen.

PLEASE DON'T TURN AWAY.

Although I sit in a silent world,

Where night combines with day,

Don't think that I can't hear you.

Please don't turn away.

> My memory may not be intact,
>
> My speech may be impaired,
>
> But I need to feel you hold my hand.
>
> I need to know you care.

Speak to me of happy times,

Occasions tinged with gold.

I may not have the answers

But I have my heart and soul.

> Don't look at me with tearful eyes,
>
> Or speak in despondent tone.
>
> Let us enjoy togetherness,
>
> We are not on our own.

I cannot speak the loving words,

Nor do the thoughtful deeds.

I know you grow frustrated

Tending to my needs.

But I'm trapped inside my body
And there's nothing I can do.
I also feel the anger
For the pain I'm causing you.

But someday I'll be going home,
My spirit will be set free.
And then I will gladly try to repay
All the love you have given me.

OPPOSITES

SUNSHINE
Would bring no pleasure
If it did not follow
RAIN

WELL BEING
Would mean nothing
Without a little
PAIN

The BRIGHTER SIDE
Would not be seen
Without the
DARK SIDE
Played its part.

And HAPPINESS
Would bring no joy
Without an
ACHING HEART.

WHICH ONE ARE YOU?

Some people seem to be like kites,
Flying high in the sky.
If they are not kept upon a string,
They'll fly off, by and by.

Some people are just like balloons,
Puffed up – about to burst.
Full of self-importance,
Always putting themselves first.

Some people are like wheelbarrows,
They work hard every day,
But need the aid of others
To push them all the way.

Some people tick along like clocks
Full of good works and true,
With an open face and a willing hand,
Strong and steady all day through.

Each one is different from the rest.
But which description fits you best?

I GIVE YOU

I give you the oceans in calm and storm,
With waves that dance in the air,
I give you the showers and the winds
And summer days warm and fair.
I give you the rainbow that springs from the sun,
The clouds that drift slowly by,
I give you the vision of anger and peace,
With beauty to feed the mind's eye.

I give you the buzz of the insects,
The drone of a plane overhead,
I give you a night beneath the stars,
Another snuggled warm in bed.
I give you the flowers, the bushes and trees,
The birds and the beasts of the field,
I give you a crop of wishes and dreams,
With the pleasure each harvest will yield.

I give you a heart to fill up with love,
The chance of a life free from cares,
All these things I gladly will give,
If you will give Me your prayers.

THE GARDEN

I sit in a beautiful garden,
With one who attends the crop;
The grass is always lush and green,
The blossoms never drop.

The plants are varied and many,
Their fragrance heady and sweet,
It's a garden exquisite and peaceful,
Where Souls who have passed can meet.

It's a vision of glorious colour,
Topped by a sunset of gold,
Where the days are sunny but never too warm,
And the nights are never too cold.

My aches and pains have vanished,
All worry and sorrow have gone.
My earthly body is finished
But my spirit is living on.

Picture me in this garden,
With this wonderful world at my feet,
And know, when it's your turn to join me,
It is here we will finally meet.

SOMEWHERE

SOMEWHERE there's a lonely soul
        In the middle of a crowd.
SOMEWHERE there's a helping hand
        If they were not so proud.

SOMEWHERE there's a someone
        Who gathers clouds of grey.
SOMEWHERE there's another
Who can brighten any day.

SOMEWHERE sun is shining,
        While here is darkest night.
SOMEWHERE a prayer is answered
        By a guiding light.

SOMEWHERE war is raging,
        Bringing fear and death and pain.
SOMEWHERE there's a haven
        Where peace and silence reign.

SOMEWHERE there's a being
        Who dwells in realms above,
And gives us all the knowledge that
        SOMEWHERE there is love.

"WHY ME?"

"Why me?" I hear you asking, many times a
day. – "Why is it when I turn to God, He
seems to turn away? – He must know the pain
I suffer! He must have seen my tears! – So
why does God ignore me? Let my prayers fall
on deaf ears?"

ANSWER

God always listens to you, hearing every word
you pray. – He knows how much you suffer
and He never turns away. – But have you
stopped to listen when God has tried to speak?
– Perhaps the answers that He gives are not
the ones you seek.

He may pour rain upon your head, but after
rain comes sun, - and He will shower you with
love, to help His will be done. – So sit and list
your blessings, from the large down to the
small, - how do you think they come about?
Who instigates them all?

God speaks within your heart, my friend. His
replies are there to see. – With many reasons
to give thanks and, perhaps to ask "Why me?"

GOOD ADVICE

His instructor gave the following advice to a learner driver.

"Remember, you are in charge of your vehicle. How you drive it is up to you; you must be aware of other road users and it makes sense to treat them to the "3 Cs", caution, consideration and courtesy. Never allow yourself to be forced into making a hasty decision you may later regret. Take your time; think about what you are doing, far better to arrive five minutes late than not at all.

All vehicles need regular attention to keep them road worthy, but how you use it or abuse it is up to you. If you have it serviced regularly and don't push it beyond its limits, it will last far longer than if you neglect it".

Excellent advice for any driver and a wonderful philosophy for life.

CORNER

*That was the clue in the crossword puzzle, five letters.
I thought of various solutions – nook, cranny, alcove,
trap – none fitted so I moved onto another clue.
Suddenly, when I wasn't even trying to find the
answer, it came – angle. The corner referred to was
a shape, not a place, which was what I thought it
meant.*

*Isn't that often the way in life? We get a set idea in
our minds, and can see no farther. Only when we
stop looking does our vision clear, showing us things
as they really are; not as we think they should be.*

*We all are guilty of trying too hard at times, attacking
problems with such frenzy we make no progress at
all. More likely make things worse growing tired and
frustrated into the bargain.*

*I found the answer to my clue by looking at it from a
different 'angle'. Perhaps if we all tried doing that
with our lives from time to time, not only would we
find the answers to our questions, but actually
become better people because of it.*

PARABLE

A tramp sat on a park bench, legs sprawled, arms folded, watching some children playing with their mother. A man in a suit, tie and highly polished shoes sat down nearby, unfolded his paper and began reading.

"Any good news today?" the tramp asked.

The man ignored him.

"The world's still in one piece, so I suppose that's something."

The man shuffled his paper with a grunt of annoyance.

"Life's wonderful really" philosophised the tramp. "Warm sunshine, the scent of flowers, children playing. God's in His heaven all's right with the world. Isn't that what they say?"

"I am trying to read my paper" stated the man.

There was silence for a moment as the tramp watched the children, smiling at their antics. "What will you do tonight?" he queried.

"Mind your own business" was the irate reply.

"Oh, I'm not prying," explained the tramp, "I only asked because it's such a glorious day and you appear to be missing it behind your paper."

Again the man ignored him.

"I suppose you're a busy man," he continued. "Not much time to yourself".

"Some of us work for a living" was the scathing response. "And yes, I am a very busy man. My lunch hour is my only break." He paused before adding "unlike some".

The tramp sat quietly, pondering the words, watching the happy little group at play. "I might not have your money or possessions" he said " but at least I can relax." Then with a shrug of his shoulders, he stood up, stretched himself, said, "enjoy your paper" and walked away.

The man lowered his paper, frowning at the back of the tramp. Laughter from the children caught his attention, just as the sun shone golden lights on their hair.

FORGIVENESS

"Forgiveness brings its own rewards". An old and true adage which is easier to say than do. Much simpler to nurse the grudge, keeping it healthy, allowing it to survive.

Yet forgiveness is as old as life itself. When Eve ate the forbidden fruit in the Garden of Eden, God did not disown her or physically punish her. Her punishment was to live with her mistake.

Many of us do things we regret, and would gladly right them if we could. We expect people to understand and accept our failings, yet we cannot always accept theirs.

Loving and forgiving may not be easy, but it is far healthier and happier than hating or harbouring grudges.

God teaches us to love one another. In the Lord's Prayer we ask: "Forgive us our trespasses". And He always does. Perhaps we should all try a little harder to follow His example.

The following piece was part of an exercise at an inspirational writer's weekend. We were given a word and asked to interpret what that word meant to us.

DIAMOND

"Diamonds are a girl's best friend" was the first thing that came to mind. But diamonds, like people, have many facets and like people none is really perfect.

Diamonds are an element of beauty much sought after, yet they have hardness beyond compare.

Some people are referred to as "rough diamonds" meaning they are good people but not as polished or refined as they could be

For centuries diamonds have been a token of love: women crave them, men have died for them, wars have raged because of them. Never have so many done so much for so little.

With a bit of effort we all could be diamonds; lighting other's lives with love. Then what a much better world this would be.

  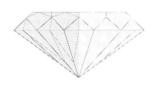

AS YE SOW SO SHALL YE REAP.

*"What goes around, comes around." A modern
adage used by many people, usually in reference to
someone who has hurt or done a bad turn to
somebody else.*

*We all know people who gossip; who never have a
good word to say about anyone and would never
lend a helping hand unless there was something to
gain for themselves. Yet those same people, should
they become victims rather than perpetrators, will
send out piteous cries of "Why me? What have I
done to deserve this?"*
"God pays his debts" might be the answer.

*It is hard to be forgiving when we have been hurt,
but nevertheless essential for our growth. By
harbouring grudges and nursing old wounds, we
cannot heal ourselves or let our souls progress.
But surround that hurt in love and light and that
pain will ease. Say a prayer for the person
causing the pain-for they obviously need help-and
you will receive help yourself.*

Sowing seeds of jealousy, bitterness and doubt will harvest misery, heartache and frustration. Sowing seeds of friendship, compassion and understanding will harvest love, light and laughter. So consider the crop you want from life and sow the seeds accordingly.

GOD'S GIFT

If you owned the most precious treasure in the entire world, what would you do with it? Would you protect it, making sure it was kept at the correct temperature? Would you clean it and put its beauty on display for all to admire? Would you be pleased and proud that you possessed such an item?

Of course you would. And the simple fact is that you do own just such a marvellous thing, the most wondrous creation of all time-the human's body.

No engineer could ever invent or design a machine capable of doing everything the body can. It has a built-in warning system against cold or heat and adjusts itself accordingly. It repairs itself following damage or mismanagement. It has its own powerhouse and sewage system, works twenty-four hours a day and never goes on strike or breaks down unless we mistreat it-something we frequently do by polluting it with smoke, alcohol or drugs. Sometimes we starve it of rest and recuperation or fail to feed it correctly, and then moan because it will not work to its full capacity.

Our bodies are a gift from God. Each one is a masterpiece; a temple for the soul, committed to our care for the duration of our stay on earth. Like life itself we only get one to do with what we will, it must make sense, therefore, to treat it with reverence and respect, always remembering it is the greatest and most precious asset we will ever possess.

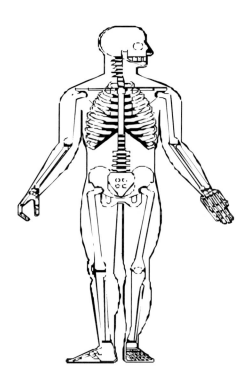

THE GOOD, THE BAD
AND
THE INBEEWEEN

Commenting to a friend that I was going to
church she grinned requesting:
"Say one for me."

"I frequently do," I replied.

This time she laughed. "I see. So you think
I'm that bad, do you?"

Isn't it strange how some people think only the "Bad"
need prayers? The "Good" need them just as much,
if not more.

The "Good" are the first ones there when help,
comfort or support is needed; they offer a listening-
ear, a comforting shoulder, a helping hand, such
things are expected of them. Should they fall down on
the job, refuse, just once, they are almost considered
guilty of the ultimate sin.

So, yes, they do need our prayers for
encouragement and strength to do all their good
works and stick to the "straight and true path".

The "Bad" also need prayers to help them see the error of their ways and to steer them from the wrong path to the right one. But how do you actually determine "Bad"? The dictionary has it as unpleasant, rotten, unfit, and of poor quality, and wicked. Yet how many times do we read of prisoners, of all categories, raising funds to pay for operations or to send a sick child on holiday?

So even in the worst of us there is an element of good and that, I think, is the part that needs prayers.

So next time you tell someone you will say a prayer for them and they respond with: "So you think I'm that bad?"

How nice to reply: "No. But I do think you're that good".

God Bless.

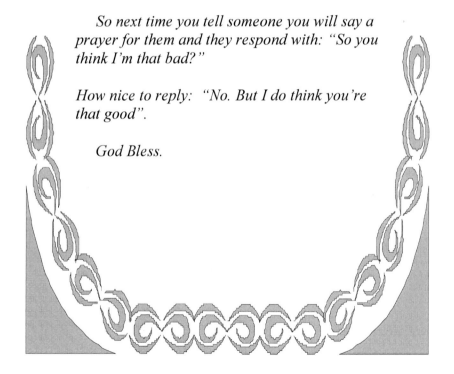

THE INNER VOICE

It is never easy to look into our own souls to see the person within. Sometimes we judge others just by looking at them, but we cannot judge ourselves. We can find fault with others; what they say, what they do, how they conduct themselves, yet we never fault ourselves. We may say we know we are not perfect, but still cannot find the flaws or try to correct them if we do.

We can offer advice to others, helping them, teaching them, yet we look to others for that same assistance, that same leadership when we need guidance. What we know can help others, does not appear to work for us.

Why?

Because we lack faith in our own abilities. We think others know more than us, are wiser, more experienced. Yet we prove when we help others, that we are just as capable, as understanding and as knowledgeable as anybody else is.

We need to believe in ourselves. Be ready to learn by our mistakes and listen to the inner voice-the instinctive reaction, the gut feeling or intuition- the personal warning system that tries to guide us. We all have it and should learn to listen to it, yet so often we ignore it, frequently regretting it when we do.

We are responsible for our own lives. We are given choices, we make the decisions, and with the aid of the inner voice we can achieve great things and become better, more confident people.

Your inner voice can be your saviour and your teacher. So start today. Look into your soul, hear what it has to say to you, listen carefully and, most importantly, have faith.

SMILE

A SMILE

Is the sunbeam of the soul,

Lighting up the eyes,

Transforming the face.

A SMILE

Scatters gloom,

Lines clouds with silver,

And sends bright rays

All over the place.

A SMILE

Costs nothing

Yet counts for so much.

Its effect remains a long while.

Nothing glows warmer,

Or makes friends quicker,

Than the brilliance of

A SMILE.

DENTAL DILEMA

I visited the dentist for my teeth had got an ache.

But even at the thought of it

My hands began to shake.

My mouth was dry; my palms were wet.

I'm a coward there's no doubt.

But I'd sooner have a baby

Than have a tooth pulled out.

So I told this to the dentist, who said, with patient air,

"Make your mind up, Madam,

And I'll adjust the chair".

MODELLED ON PERFECTION.

I was modelled on perfection,
But, alas the model failed.
I was born with shining beauty,
But in later years it paled.

The light that shone within my eyes
Has gradually gone out,
I suffer with arthritis
And I've got a touch of gout.

My waistline has expanded,
Like the ever-growing world,
My legs are long and gangly,
While my hair is short and curled.

The brain that once worked overtime,
Has dimmed its little light,
The teeth rest nightly in a cup,
While my eyes go out of sight.

I used to dance all evening,
Kick my legs above my head.
But now I sit and watch T.V.,
And then go off to bed.

The years have really taken toll,
All the signs are there.
I've got wrinkles,
I've got crow's feet,
I've got silver in my hair.

But I wouldn't change a minute
Of any ache or pain,
For their cause was quite enjoyable,
And will not come again.

So happily I'll carry on
Until God cries "enough".
And if anyone objects to that
All I can say is "tough"!

DOMESTIC BLUES

I often have a grumble
'cos the oxo cubes won't crumble
While me apple crumble
Burns and sticks together.
Me sponges go rock hard,
Me rock cakes I discard,
Sometimes I reach the end of me tether.
I bought a set of scales;
I bought a mixer, too,
But they don't make a difference
To the cooking that I do.
I can't even follow recipes.
I'm in a proper stew.
So what's a girl to do, I ask yer?

I tried domestic science
But couldn't manage the appliance,
And I put the teacher in a proper spin,
When the cooker I was using
Suffered culinary bruising
And she had to call the service chappy in.
He told us that the cooker
Had gone into a decline.
Said he couldn't understand it.
He had others working fine.
I could only smile sweetly,
Well, I knew the fault was mine.
But what's a girl to do, I ask yer?

Me husband's full of quips,
He's fed up with fish and chips
And he'd like a suet pud put on the table.
The kids would like a pie.
I tell 'em "So would I
And I'd make the blessed things if I was able."

I've been a martyr to that kitchen
Yet me future looked real bleak.
But now, at last, I think I've found
The answer that I seek.
I've booked hubby cooking lessons.
Yes. He's starting them next week.
Well, what's a girl to do, I ask yer?

OUR SON

He was my son when a baby
And needed pushing in his pram.
He was my son when he started school
And failed his first exam.

He's my son if he's cheeky
Or ever misbehaves.
He's my son when he's poorly
And some attention craves.

He's my son if he's lazy
Or doesn't pull his weight.
He's my son if he's dirty
And his clothes are in a state.

He's my son when he can't get up.
He's my son late at night.
He's my son every time he's wrong,
But then, I'm never right.

So what I'd like to know is why?
When his talents do shine through,
Does OUR SON become quite special?
And exclusive to you?

"WHOOPEE!"

I've found meself a feller,
Dark and handsome, slightly grey,
I'm gonna lock him in a room
And throw the key away.
Then I'm gonna love him,
On the bed and on the floor,
And when he thinks I'm finished,
I'll do it all some more.

I'm gonna let him have it
Like a woman, who's possessed,
Then I'll mark him out of ten
On how he's passed the test.

I do hope he's got stamina,
Is virile and quite strong,
I've got some catching up to do,
I've been without too long.
I just can't wait to get him
In that room all to myself,
No longer will I be the
Shrinking violet on the shelf.

I think perhaps I'll call him,
Let him know what I'm about.
What's this?…An answer phone?
Cor! Just my luck, he's out.

WALKIES

My mistress takes me for a walk
But, well, I wouldn't mind,
I like to get a move on
But she will lag behind.
Sometimes she takes forever.
It's really quite frustrating.
So I exercise my nose a bit
And sniff round while I'm waiting.

> But my mistress doesn't like that,
> She makes chastising remarks,
> It seems one shouldn't poke ones nose
> Into other canine's marks.
> So I try to be a good dog,
> I don't like to hear her moan,
> So I squat me bot upon the kerb
> To leave traces of my own.

But she doesn't like that either
As, with a threatening mutter,
She drags me, almost choking,
And plonks me in the gutter.
Sometimes I sit for hours
While she shops or stops to chat.
And I often get to wonder
Why we ever left the flat.

> I'm not allowed out on my own,
> I'm from the "upper crust".
> Even my beaus are chosen
> So I have to mate on trust.

But once we get into the park
That's where I have my fun.
I swim in the lake; I chase the ducks,
I roll and bark and run.

But if I find another dog
To join me in my play,
My mistress calls me to her side
Until he goes away.
And when she feels she's had enough
She calls a halt to me.
It really is dog's life
Being pedigree.

But I suppose it proves she loves me,
And I should be glad of that,
For our walks may not be perfect
But she never takes the cat.

PROGRESS

From trolleys and trams
To long traffic jams
We've advanced in the name of progress.
It was slower by far
But is it quicker by car
With our highways in such a damned mess?

Hansom cabs roamed the street
With the driver discreet,
And lovers could sit cheek to cheek.
But today when they hire
A mini cab driver
He hears every word that they speak.

Though much was on ration
Folk still managed fashion
With ladies in tight, lace up stays.
While the men wore cravats,
Top hats and spats
And visited operas and plays.

Chaperones were a must,
No indulging in lust,
Such feelings were locked out of sight.
But now they have trials
With bawdy, bed smiles,
And never think twice of their plight.

A day at the races,
In flat cap and braces,
And handkerchief tied in a knot,
Where a bob on the winner
Could buy a days dinner,
Was better than now at Ascot.

The 'sixpenny flicks',
Roy Rogers, Tom Mix,
Was always a must for each kid.
But now it's not strange
When the mums get no change
After giving their children five quid.

Oh, those were the days
With their magical ways,
And some for their passing do morn.
But such grief's not for me,
For, my friends, you must see,
They happened before I was born.

NELLY'S PUSSY

Nelly's little pussy
Had an ear filled up with wax
So Nelly thought she'd clean it out
To help it to relax.
But she hadn't any cotton buds
So Nelly, like a fool,
Filled her pussy's ear hole
With a wad of cotton wool.
She rubbed it very gently
And she wiggled it about
But then, to Nelly's horror,
Found she couldn't get it out.

So off to the vets ran Nelly
Where the fault was quickly found,
And Nelly's bit of folly
Had her forking out five pound.
But still it wasn't over
For Nelly had to wait
To see if when she went again
It would cost another eight.
But Nelly was so sorry
For the sad mistake she made
That she thought of buying pussy
A little hearing aid.

But the moral to this story
Is to always keep your cool.
And never poke your pussy
With a wad of cotton wool.

GRANNY AND HER SKATEBOARD.

She glides down the road with the greatest of ease
Strapped to her skateboard at ankles and knees.
She whizzes past houses, she rushes past shops
Ignoring the red lights where everyone stops.
She wheelies and side surfs round cars and parked trucks,
Doing slalom and kick tails or mad Daffy Ducks.
She zooms down the street at breathtaking pace,
With two dozen school kids giving her chase.

Her hands sore from pushing, her face turning red,
As the wind blows her skirt right over her head.
Feeling embarrassed, and courting disaster,
Her arms move like windmills pushing her faster.
What is she doing? Where is she going?
With her eyes hid from view and her knickers all showing.
If she don't hit a tree, and she makes no mistakes.
She'll go home with her skateboard and fit it with brakes.

57

STARTING ART

I started art last Friday,
Well, I thought I'd have a go.
I see myself as a Constable,
Or creating Art Nouveaux.

So there I sat with board on lap,
My pencil at the ready,
Holding it the way he said,
My hand a mite unsteady.

First I had to draw a box
Then fill it in with lines.
Apparently when starting art,
You do this several times.

I drew so many boxes
I quite hated the sight,
So I thought to give my left a rest
And draw some with my right.

When I asked him what he thought
Do you know what that man said?
That he preferred the latest ones.
Was I sure I was left handed?

Well, I'm sure he meant it kindly,
But I thought he had a cheek.
Still, I'll go again on Friday
And report back here next week.

THE TATTY TWO-PIECE

Oh, I've really done it now folks,
I broke the rules, no doubt.
I stupidly threw the other half's
Tatty two-piece out.

And he does so love that outfit
He's worn it like no other.
If you heard the way he speaks of it
You'd think it was his lover.

The sleeves are hanging on by threads,
The lining's falling out.
The trousers are held up with string,
And his knees and elbows sprout.

I said I'd buy another
From the Oxfam down the street.
And what his answer was to that
I simply can't repeat.

So I fished it from the ragbag
And his face lit up with glee.
But I'm not sure that I've acted right
For now he lectures me.

At least when he was sulking
He couldn't have a nag.
So as soon as I can grab that suit,
It's straight back in the bag.

THE TWILIGHT ZONE

When I reach the 'Twilight Zone'
Will I face it on my own?
When I'm haggard, bent and grey
Will you want me anyway?

When my teeth are in a cup,
My rheumatism's playing up,
When my waistline's out of sight
And my eyes come off at night,

When my hearing's on the blink,
If I shake through too much drink,
When I wear a woolly vest,
And Vick lies heavy on my chest,
When my joints all creak and groan,
Will you leave me on my own?

But if I do the things I should

And promise to be really good,

Stick to a diet, stay off gin,

Greet adversity with a grin,

If I stay chastened, trim and nifty,

Will you still want me when I'm fifty?

PRE MED. BLUES

There I lay upon the bed,
Dosed to the eyeballs with pre med.,
When a little old lady wandered along,
And asked us if we'd like a song.
I thought "how kind", 'til the silly old cow,
Gave us her version of "Who's sorry now?"

A TIGHT SITUATION

I had a ladder in my tights
You should have seen the size!
It started off around my knee
And worked up to my thighs.
It ran down to my ankle,
It spread out round my calf,
And when it reached up to my waist
The damned things fell in half.

WHY?

Why is it, when my home is a wreck,
After a lazy spell,
I get a stream of visitors
Ringing at my bell?

But, when it's looking lovely,
With everything in place,
And I would welcome callers,
There is not a single trace.

COLD COMFORT

It was one day in September,
As I very well remember,
I was sitting in the pictures – one and nine's,
When you glanced along the row,
It set my heart aglow,
And very soon we sat, your hand in mine.

    Clark Gable graced the screen,
    With Vivian Leigh as queen,
    I sighed with envy as I watched them kiss.
    Then I felt your mouth on mine
    And, for a short moment of time,
    I knew the warmth, the passion and the bliss.

But it ended, sad to say,
When the ice creams came our way,
It was then that the passion quickly froze.
As the cornet came to grief,
It pulled out your false teeth,
And left a lump of ice cream on your nose.

    You put them back real quick,
    But then said you felt sick,
    And to the gents you hurried away.
    While I felt quite sorry for you,
    That's the last time that I saw you.
    If I'd waited, love, I'd still be there today.

So I watched the film alone
Then wandered slowly home,
Reflecting on a love that was no more.
But I've learned my lesson, so,
When next viewing with a beau,
There'll be no ice creams for us. And that's for sure.

'POOR OLD FRED'.

This is the tale of 'poor old Fred',
Whose Christmas drink went to his head.
His wife had to put him into bed,
Where Fred slept, just like a baby.

He lay in bed, a bucket in place,
A deathly pallor upon his face,
His wife sat up with him, just in case.
But Fred slept, just like a baby.

Next morning she struggled out of bed,
He needed aspirin for his head,
And so she waited on 'poor old Fred'
Who'd slept, just like a baby.

She dished the presents from round the tree,
Cooked the dinner and made the tea.
She ran herself ragged so that he
Could sleep in, just like a baby.

She played with the children with their toys,
Insisting that they limit their noise.
All day long she kept her poise,
While Fred slept, just like a baby.

At eight in the evening he ventured down
And said he was going into town.
She used a saucepan as a crown.
And Fred slept, just like a baby.

FAIRY ON THE CHRISTMAS TREE

"I'm the fairy on the Christmas tree,

Me tights are torn and tattered.

They keep me in a box, you know,

So now me wings are shattered.

Me halo's gone all wonky,

Me wand's gone on the blink,

Me dress, once brightly coloured,

Is now a dirty pink.

> The santas and the snowmen
>
> That they put upon the tree,
>
> Are all placed on with loving care,
>
> They're not slung on like me.
>
> At night I hear them laughing,
>
> And the chocolate soldiers stare,
>
> And all I can do is blush with shame
>
> At me tatty underwear.

Last year the baby grabbed me,

Screwed me head and made me wince,

Then me arm came out of its socket

And it hasn't been right since.

The only part I did enjoy

Was when the lanterns went to pot.

Well, it's no fun with your legs lit up,

They get so bloomin' hot.

What a way to earn a living, eh?

Working once a year.

Looking down on all the fun

With a branch stuck up your rear.

Oh, look out. The décor's finished.

The wine is flowing free.

It's my turn once again folks.

It's me for the top of the tree.

HAPPY NEW YEAR

NEW YEAR'S RESOLUTION!

With the New Year now upon us
And the old year out of sight,
Once again we have the chance
To put the world to right.

To put an end to violence,
To still the anger deep.
To give future generations
The chance of peaceful sleep.

This year let us all resolve
To love each other more,
And to venture onto pathways
We have never walked before.

For each day is a challenge
To be met with strength and pride,
Knowing that the good Lord
Is walking at our side.

Let the light that lives within
Each one of us, shine out,
Filling the world with laughter,
Dispelling fears and doubt.

This years resolutions
Should be filled with thoughts of others.
No race, no creed, no colour bar,
In God's eyes we are brothers.

Let's extend the hand of friendship,
Be honest and sincere,
Fill our hearts and minds with good
And God Bless our New Year.

SMILE PLEASE

If you whinge or weep and moan
You'll always spend your days alone.

But keep a smile on your face
And you'll have friends in every place.

SEASONS GREETINGS

May you have the Light of Love,

Glow within your heart,

To warm you throughout Christmas

And help the New Year start.